Rooted and Reduced to Dust

poems by

Ivy Raff

Finishing Line Press
Georgetown, Kentucky

Rooted and Reduced to Dust

Copyright © 2024 by Ivy Raff
ISBN 979-8-88838-376-6 First Edition
All rights reserved under International and Pan-American Copyright Conventions. No part of this book may be reproduced in any manner whatsoever without written permission from the publisher, except in the case of brief quotations embodied in critical articles and reviews.

ACKNOWLEDGMENTS

The author gratefully acknowledges the publications in which these poems first appeared:

A version of "The Bicycle Speaks," anthologized in *Spectrum: Poetry Celebrating Identity* (Renard Press, 2022)
"I Once Loved Yehuda," "Pantoum for a Eulogy," and "Thank-You Note to My Father's Depression," all in *Toasted Cheese Literary Magazine*, Vol. 22, Issue 3, September 2022
"Deep-Winter Days" in *t'ART Magazine*, Issue 4, September 2022
"On Not Speaking My Own Native Language" in *Exist Otherwise*, inaugural issue, September 2022

Publisher: Leah Huete de Maines
Editor: Christen Kincaid
Cover Art: Caitlin Cartwright
Author Photo: Ivy Raff
Cover Design: Elizabeth Maines McCleavy

Order online: www.finishinglinepress.com
also available on amazon.com

Author inquiries and mail orders:
Finishing Line Press
PO Box 1626
Georgetown, Kentucky 40324
USA

Contents

Now-speak 1

The Bicycle Speaks 2

Thank-You Note to My Father's Depression 3

Pantoum for a Eulogy 5

Last Letter to My Grandmother, an Accused Narcissist 6

My Father Never Stopped 8

Ivy Has Problems, They Said (1996/2021) 9

Deep-Winter Days 11

Where Did It All Go (1976/2016) 12

At Daugava River, Aleksandr Looks Me Up and Down and Asks
    How I Came to Be Here 14

A Memoirist Asks What Desert I Will Have to Enter to Tell My Story ... 16

I Once Loved Yehuda 17

On Not Speaking My Own Native Language 18

Far Rockaway Is a Ghost 19

Heaven and earth conspire that everything which has been, be rooted and reduced to dust. Only the dreamers, who dream while awake, call back the shadows of the past and braid nets from the unspun thread.

—Isaac Bashevis Singer

Now-speak

*my father and his parkinsons now speak
in departures   his words are flesh of trans
figurations   a persevering beast with vectors
for thighs, a cliff of collar bone
a face of no affect salt as sentence*

the last time I saw my Grandpa
Reuben was December 1960, right

before he died they told me to wave
good bye that was

the last time I saw him

in a hospital bed in Brooklyn he was fifty-seven
people didn't know to take care of themselves

in those days   he had trouble
finding workers so Grandma Shirley said *I'll help*

you I remember her schlepping
bathtubs up the stairs

The Bicycle Speaks

Far Rockaway, New York

Once I carried the boy over Marine Park Bridge on summer evenings
when the sun sent rays turned whitened rods glinting to the surface of me.
I was lightening bolts under the boy's dungarees, and I was his joy. His father
polished me, swiped me slick with chemicals to combat the rust. Only the best

for his boy of few pleasures and fewer mates at school. At PS 102 they tittered
he looked like an alien, plastic cords poking from the hearing-box affixed
to his thrush-ribbed chest, sliding into his ear canals, transporting sound
from speakers along his personal air waves. On me the boy was king. I held

his birdweight, quickened in time with his blood, slowed when he burned
ravenous or when August roast coaxed the salt from him. The boy in the cowboy
hat and bolo tie. The boy with the gap in his gum-tab teeth. The boy who sopped
his mother's borscht and brisket drippings with good Jew rye. The boy who didn't

speak a word until his seventh birthday, when he tore the shining giftbow off
my handlebars and set the tip of his tongue to the back of his dungeon gate
teeth and mouthed his first sentence: *Thank You.* Voice, untainted by human
    timbre,
feathered open.

Thank-You Note to My Father's Depression

For the moments in his life you permitted
to rest uncomplicated. For when he griddled

sandwiches in Morningside Heights
to put himself through Columbia. His grilled

cheese was so damn good I can only think it sparked
pleasure, learning to smear the butter

on the outsides of slices and flip the melt
in the right fragment of time between golden brown

and too-burnt. For letting his teeth crack the crisp.
He thought, *Hey this is good*, a flash of mild,

surprised satisfaction. For stepping back so he could
stay engrossed, sky-hued eyes trained

on his father's work-arched spine as he fixed
the engine on the Impala, mechanical mind

figuring and integrating. Something that makes
sense, finally, a car engine. For letting him be,

in the summertimes he could steal away from you,
a little boy in a straw cowboy hat and bolo tie

in the shoot-'em-up sixties, skipping along the quiet
lapping line of Jamaica Bay, swatting away mosquitoes

between bouts of becoming engrossed again, in the twitchings
of new guppies. He sounded delighted even pronouncing

the word guppies, babies wriggled on his tongue. For that time
you desisted enough for his brain to invent

a similar word—iggy—to describe his chest, warm,
protected, snug-feeling in a thick vest in winter.

And he'd physically snuggle when he said the word iggy,
bear down on his ribs, close his eyes and break a hot chocolate

smile, transported back to relief from a slushy Queens
December in the seventies, everything tinted brown with cold

decay. You let him find, despite yourself, a kernel of warmth
alive at his core. Iggy, his own word. His own Yiddish.

Pantoum for a Eulogy

We children arrived at the retirement home
after her travels in China. We found Rho in Marco Polo mode
returned from her Far East sojourn laden with goods.
She spread them on that lipstick-red living room carpet.

After her travels in China, we found Rho in Marco Polo mode
gifting a rainbow of stone-inlaid bangles to my mother.
She spread them on that lipstick-red living room carpet:
mechanized toys for the boychildren, flat-smiled dolls for me.

Gifted a rainbow of stone-inlaid bangles from my mother,
I spoke Rhoda's eulogy decades later to the tear-sliced faces of my aunts
    remembering
mechanized toys for the boychildren, flat-smiled dolls for me.
Seeds in the wind! We never think they will blow back to us.

I spoke Rhoda's eulogy decades later. The tear-sliced faces of my aunts
    remembered
we children arriving at the retirement home
as seeds in the wind they never thought would blow back to them
until we'd returned from our Far East sojourns, laden with goods.

Last Letter to My Grandmother, an Accused Narcissist

Your children said you were a narcissist. I wish I could
have asked you how you respond to that charge.

Your husband held an M.S. Ed. from NYU and his own mother
who also threw pots at the cabinets—did he bet you were a narcissist

too? I remember him barking at you to shut up your small
talk with pink-aproned waitresses at the pancake house,

or when you oohed and aahed with great lingual flourishes
on the walking paths at Sequoia National Park. Everyone else

stepped silent between three-thousand-year-old trees. You never
conceived the coffee waitresses carried existed for other tables,

or mothers in airport bathrooms wanted to change diapers and not
hear about your handsome AirForceDoctorSon. How did you really

feel in 1972, on the London vacation for which Poppa scrimped
on his principle's paycheck, when he told you he peers into every blue-eyed

late 20-something's face for traces of his own, of the war baby
whose mother he left when he came home to you? I wish I asked you

while you were alive. I didn't, because my mother said you didn't want us
to know. You wanted us to believe the fresh detergent

on the crew neck sweaters, the gleaming golf clubs, the starched shorts
he wore to convey purity to his massage clients. You wanted us

to love a man who didn't exist, the way the people you love don't exist
but as pictures in your mind, slant reflections in slimming mirrors.

I wish I would have respected your wishes less, and my mother's too.
We could have healed together from your pain

of not having married Paul Newman. We could have cried together
for his war nurse abandoned, or for men's clandestine babymaking. I'm sorry

I didn't know this then: comfort is crutch. But goodbye, Rhoda. You
should know that picture of you vamping on Brighton Beach at age fifteen
   lives on

a white bookcase in my kitchen in Detroit, a city incomprehensible to you.
Your svelte thigh stretched long on the sand, your flowered scarf

knotted perfectly at your forehead, protecting the corkscrew curls from
curing in the sun. I realize now your complaints about your dry hair lasted

nine decades. I remember long rows of heady oils and creams
on your vanity, carefully placed Easter eggs. I remember Aunt Roberta—

Jerry's Second Wife, as your generation exclusively called her—applying
Clarins Red Hot Chili Pepper to my seven-year-old kissy lips before

the stark naked bulbs pearled around that mirror
while your old friends roared with nostalgia,
picked over the turkey carcass in the formal dining room.

Your children said you were a narcissist, and you were, and I
wish I could have asked you how you respond to that charge.

My Father Never Stopped

talking about the summer of 1981.
His marriage still-starched lace, his children
unmade. Like Texans he loved the potential
of our fetus-selves, oily cells interred
in his lawful wife, not yet screaming, not yet
mouths, not yet making crumbs of the kitchen.

Ivy Has Problems, They Said (1996/2021)

1

I'm just *trying to raise* my boys,
my mother begged. I'd shut myself
in the bedroom with the blushing gingham
wallpaper cut around a bay window.
No country for thirteen-year-old girls
after a rape, just desert highways without exits,
masses lined roadside holding protest
signs against her poison.

2

Detroit is thick socks and door locks, everyone shut
in their private cold. No sun for months. The river
doesn't glitter for swimmers. This, America's Scandinavia

bears reminding (myself) I was born
in a ninety-three degree September. Fields stretched
below the windows of Rio Grande Regional Hospital's

delivery ward. *We were pioneers!* said my father of the year
1981, of a place the Church disappeared Sepinpacam gatherers
centuries before.

3

Fifteen years later his daughter is a pariah about town
and mothers cluck over the phone, *Lisa* or *Lauren*
or *Clarissa can't come over. Ivy has problems.* And I don't
know yet that slut shaming little girls is a time-honored tactic.
We say *that bitch is crazy* to distance our culpability. This is how
we execute it, and execute her. I don't know yet. I begin to fear
my body's in-side but it doesn't feel like fear at first. It feels like fire
only fire. Elemental, uncomplicated. Flying light inside
sparked against convexities of ribs, burning little round holes
into lungs and heart, cigarette butts on couch cushions.
I wouldn't have said I was afraid then—I wasn't scared of *shit*.
But boy, was I running.

4

I fear the body's in-sides. In the dream I dive off
skyscrape cranium, all hair and wind,
with wings affixed at first, then shucked off
when my feet pad sidewalk and I advance
through the megalopolis among everyone else
and their bodies too.

I fear sea monsters, fjord-lurk, dark
venom of waterway. I wake to Detroit
winter.

5

All my talk of Oneness: They
with their capital T are still Everyone
Else to me. All this community
nonsense. I've been bluffing.
I have no hometown.
I buck like a mustang when any place
tries to claim me. This after pining for a cliff
I wouldn't be asked to hurl myself over
for the greater good.

6

I'm just *trying to raise my* boys,
my mother begged.
I shut myself.

Deep-Winter Days

On the deep-winter days I raise
the white flags   I pull my feet into the soft
            twin arcs inside these legs—
                my own flesh as bunker. I burrow
under uncovered down duvet stained
with feathered pen marks from writing in bed,
toss implements aside to make love, then
forget   them, Bic hidden
in the trenches   I moan and toss
        On the deep winter days of ice-fluffs
float from the sky   with nowhere
        in particular to go   I hear the air's
            silence, the ceasing
of Lafayette's traffic. I hear my pen glide
on the page, my grandmother's engagement ring
scratching paper like a memory, like boot heels
            dragged across her *dacha's*[1] wooden floor
            She was nineteen when she married,
with spaghetti arms and crackable collar bone
        I am nearly forty and wear her
engagement ring on my ruddy pinkie. She would never
have believed I'd live in my man's Midwest, a place less
        desirable a volcano's mouth: at least
            there's fire at Fuji.
        But in the dead-deep of winter I surrender
to the mattress   I let sleep
gather my eyelids like the drift, and I peer into Ontario
across the river for the perennial slash in the breath-gray
sky.

---

[1] A dacha is a Russian country cottage. Unlike in the US, where second homes are for the rich, virtually all Russian urbanites have a dacha.

Where Did It All Go (1976/2016)

Ain't too much sadder than an artist
who never became himself. My father will die
in his small body of paintings, abandoned
for sensible things: a wife, a three-bedroom ranch.

He entered his lithographs
in a competition at Columbia once. The pieces received
harsh criticism from a beloved professor. My father never
held a paint brush again.

I wonder now what became of the art supplies
that must have clustered in a corner, what became
of my father's chalk and his charcoal,
his tubes of acrylics and their rainbow-splatter brushes.

Did he bundle them in a sheet, lug them, clandestine,
to the bin by the basement stairs? Or would that have sloshed
his heart in a vice? Would he have asked his mother
to dispose of them, breezed the question through

the screen door as it whined shut behind him
on his way to the A train. Would he have invented
a reason for the ejection—*they expired, they're a bad
batch, losing color*—lied to her?

I can't imagine he cried to her, let his eyes squeeze salt dreams
before my Russian grandmother, who knew
something about crushings and found us all frivolous.

>Hunkered for Snowpocalypse, Aaron asked me
why Daddy stopped painting
so I told him. *He fucking quit?
What the fuck?* My even-toned, affable
brother sizzled up his spine-bolt,
a chain usually bowed over
a keyboard, editing other people's
films. He popped a clenched fist.

Before he could slam it on the bar, he shifted his eyes to the fist, peered at it quizzically, as if this great ovoid, hairy-knuckled insect had just flown in and hovered in the winter before his face. He opened his fingers and set his hand back down, gentle, returned to civility.

At Daugava River, Aleksandr Looks Me Up and Down and Asks How I Came to Be Here

Well, Alex, Jewish men
migrated north from Jerusalem after the destruction
of the Second Temple.

In Europe they found Gentile
wives, threw them
from the impending frying pan of early

Christianity into the fire
of O.G. monotheism.
White girls love appropriated

yoga in their Lululemons
now. Back then it was Judaism,
a sexy cult with swarthy men,

hairy chests to rest upon,
guttural accents from which to relish
spiritual and housekeeping orders.

Their descendants, over
the generations and generations
and generations ended up with an average

thirteen percent Middle Eastern DNA—
a composite great grandparent
nagging at our neurons. A certain

cerebral line of King David's descended
to be Judges in the religious
courts, codifying laws, interpreting

Talmud for the mundanities
of Diaspora life. For medieval
centuries, Frankish borders batted,

Alsace changed hands. Whims
of popes dictated Judges would live
in ghettoes, would endure corporal

punishment past curfew, childlike beatings meted
on backsides of grown men. Still they took
root here until one branch pulled up roots,

as my people are wont to do, and settled again, east
again, another border—this time between Latvia
and Lithuania. So that's the general answer

to your question, Lexy boy. I remain unable to center
or specify myself, what with the generational
history of displacement, assimilation and pogroms.

A Memoirist Asks What Desert I Will Have to Enter to Tell My Story

Desert of the czar. Desert of pogrom. Desert of Atlantic.
Of grandmother in ground, of grandmother in hold of ship,
of grandmother's clandestine marriage and kitchen table
abortions. Desert of Brighton Beach. Desert of Williamsburg.
Desert of Bedford Stuyvesant after Desert of Houston Street after
Desert of borders then-unexisted, scrubbed from Desert
of Empire. Desert of the wandered-out Jew: butchers
and tailors and timber merchants. Desert of shoulders
forever compressed, of wrists torqued back. Desert of hip,
of nerve endings, of nerves unending, of nerves beginning.
Desert of factory fires, of picket lines, of fighting for wages
and workweeks, of tenements rat-clawed. Desert of egg breads in braids,
of brined fish in jars, eyeless, matzo-plumped. Desert of soup,
and soup, and soup again. Of celery. Of beets. Of chicken bones
stretched for marrow-days. Of chicken fat rendered, roasting
pan-harvested, plopped in a jar atop the icebox. No butter
in the desert, just schmaltz already heat-proofed.

To tell my story the desert must die and move to the suburbs.
Must choose wallpaper from swatches in great hardcover sample books
while fluorescence hums overhead. To tell my story I must
forget bitter herbs, forget Yiddish poems, unsing songs. Unchant. Unbleed.
Unsubmit. Nonchalant. Relearn womanness. Reassemble
chopped lettuce into whole, crisp leaves. I must forget pants
and wrap myself homespun. I must enter
others' deserts alone: Gobi, Mojave, Sahara, Sonora.
My own Desert died, lady. My Desert drowned
in the Atlantic.

I Once Loved Yehuda

Six thousand year old man swam
from the Gulf of Aden into my
left atrium, pressed an ear to my chest
as it battered and said, *Gentile hearts
are different from ours.* Closed
his face, mewled in ecstasy as my music
echoed inside him.

Before Titus destroyed the second
temple, I looked like Yehuda, I
bound books like Yehuda, I
cracked cardamom seeds with my
molars. Two millennia later he
reoccupied Al-Quds as Yemen
convulsed with hunger pangs.
Yafa sheli, he whispers, my
beauty. And yesterday grimaced
when I stuffed the headscarf
he gifted me into my backpack.

Yehuda and I lay under
a sunbeam in Brooklyn, clean
sheets, gingered lentils softening
on the stove, far and close. With his
medicine lingering in my body dreams
wick me and my grandmother's
grandmother comes, introduces herself
as Rajchel. 'The scourge of Europe,"
governments called her when she fled.
And she bound herself to her husband
for protection. She told me to run.
Told me to run.

On Not Speaking My Own Native Language

I have questions,
questions in the only spoken language I speak,
and so the questions are themselves perversions,
distortions.

The questions are observers
By their limited and limiting nature
they cannot observe themselves.

First:
What does it mean to speak languages
separate from one's roots, and nothing else?
I know that answer, you see, but it lies in me
locked and silent, unable, unwilling to form itself,
rebelling, resisting, giving the shackles
something to scrape against.
That soulsilence has no desire to be heard,
cares not about the ears receiving the fall
of the proverbial tree in its forest—only about the ether
undulating around the spatial shift behind the crash.
Some answers deserve to rest wordless.

Second:
Since, in these languages, every word is the wrong one,
misshapen and misshaping
the language of Touch,
the language of Setting Out a Saucer of Milk for the Strays,
the language of Coming Home After Endless Turns on the Dance Floor
Then Deep Frying Whatever's in the Fridge
Before Making Love Long Into Sunrise, the language of What
They Call Passion and Care, where do these things happen?
Where do they happen?

Dys-ancestral languages translate against the will of direct experience
violate the sanctity of Sweeping the Floor in an Injured Friend's Home.
They lace What They Call Kindness with subconscious

constructs of giver to receiver. Their languages cage and are caged in clusters
of vectors. Their Word for Spiral succeeds "Downward:"
more imposed directionality still.

Far Rockaway Is a Ghost

for my grandfather, Marvin Reff

I.

Marvin's basement bears, still, gritty brown water lines six feet
under, six feet above the basement floor. After Sandy, Tupperware
bins floated on the surface, crowded around the second step leading
to the dungeon drowned, like prisoners clamoring for a meal.
My grandfather's ghost haunts me. His body
hasn't died, only he speaks of death all the time. He knows its contours
already, the way moonlight falls on its cheekbones. My grandfather
is ninety-four. He waits. He's gone from Rockaway, the house
sold to an Orthodox family, filled with children, with raisins, with generations
of another family's Jewish paraphernalia—candlesticks, challah cloth,
the special tallis, the tallis for every day. Someone else's
grandfather blesses wine there now.

Metaphor-house with a Zip code, doubled ones to start, and six-nine-one,
numbers of sharpness, numbers that dangle a hairline peninsula's tip, razor
edge of city where skyscrapers shadow blue over trestles, over big concrete
walls built to stave off the next storm. *It's not a question of whether,
but of when and how bad,* brooded Cuomo at a press conference
after Sandy. But the people of Rockaway knew this for a long time, spent
decades shoveling storm water off basement, foundation, floors.

II.

In Rockaway COVID ravaged. Marvin's
shul lost a generation in three weeks.
They'd fought in Normandy and Hoengsong, and Spring
2020 finally caught them.
The community decided, fatefully, to proceed
with Mildred's ninetieth birthday party.
They drank from the same kiddush cup.
Marvin stayed home because
my aunt and my brother screamed at him.
Nine decades an orphan, he remains
afraid of screams. He survived his first
pandemic to wish for dying all the time.

III.

Dusk-net of skin curled over ulna, drum-taut, stretched. He doesn't sag and wrinkle like other old men; he is a rubber band yet to spring, salt air-hardened, time-rusted. He curls a lip in disdain for my whole grains, my brother's rice-rolled *raw fish crap*. He eats Utz every day, brand-loyal as Jay-Z to Cartier. On porcelain incisors he crunches through dark-matted pretzel skin burnt to spec, salt diamonds from paleolithic times. My grandfather has lived to his mid-nineties on pretzels and can only speak of dying, can only speak of my grandmother who tried unsuccessfully to replace his stash of Utz with graham crackers when his doctor diagnosed high blood pressure in the mid-nineties. My grandmother is ten years dead now. Marvin survived her on pretzels. Eight months later, he shrugged off Sandy and the damages: the trees through rooftops, the mattresses strewn curbside. *This is Ha-shem's way of telling me I shoulda cleaned out that basement forty years ago.*

IV.

Assisted living now,
Long Island luxury.

*It's like a goddamn college dorm
for old people in here.*

He never goes to Bingo.
He doesn't like the walkers

all lined up by the door,
a railing to Nowhere.

I sign out at the front desk,
print Room 303.

The receptionist brightens.
My main man Marvin!

He's your favorite, right?

Girl, he's everybody's favorite.

Ivy Raff's is the author of *What Remains / Qué queda* a bilingual English/Spanish poetry collection that won the Alberola International Poetry Prize (Editorial DALYA forthcoming 2024). Her work has been anthologized in *Spectrum: Poetry Celebrating Identity, Kinship: Poems on Belonging* (Renard Press, 2022 & 2023), *London Independent Story Prize Anthology* (LISP, 2023), and *Aesthetica Creative Writing Prize Annual* (Aesthetica, 2023). Her Best of the Net-nominated work has garnered scholarship support from the Colgate Writers' Conference, Hudson Valley Writers Center, and Under the Volcano, as well as residencies with Atlantic Center for the Arts and Alaska State Parks.

Following a twenty-year career in health technology and public policy, Ivy shifted her focus to writing in 2021. She freelances as a copywriter, translator, and website designer, and serves on the editorial teams of *Reckoning*, a literary journal on environmental justice, and *Seventh Wave Magazine*. Mainly nomadic, she calls Queens, NY home.